ABBA, YOUR FATHER, SPEAKS

BOOK I

Marie-Josée Thibault

Abba, your Father, Speaks: Book I
Published by Abba Books LLC
abbabooksllc@gmail.com
Copyright © 2021 Marie-Josée Thibault

All Rights Reserved

No part of this publication may be reproduced, distributed, or transmitted in any form or by any means, including photocopying, recording, or other electronic or mechanical methods, without the prior written permission of the publisher.

1st Edition, 2021
Designed and Edited by Abba Books LLC
ISBN: 978-1-7377418-0-0

Abba Books LLC
34972 Newark Blvd, #441
Newark, CA 94560

www.abbamyfatheriloveyou.com
https://www.facebook.com/AbbaILoveYouBooks/

TABLE OF CONTENTS

PREFACE VI

I AM 1

YOU 5

PRAY 9

CHRIST JESUS OF NAZARETH 15

MY DIVINE WILL 19

HEAVEN 25

LOVE 29

MY OWN WAY 33

JOHN THE BAPTIST . . . 37

ON EARTH 41

AFTERWORD 45

ABOUT THE AUTHOR 46

ALSO BY MARIE-JOSÉE THIBAULT 47

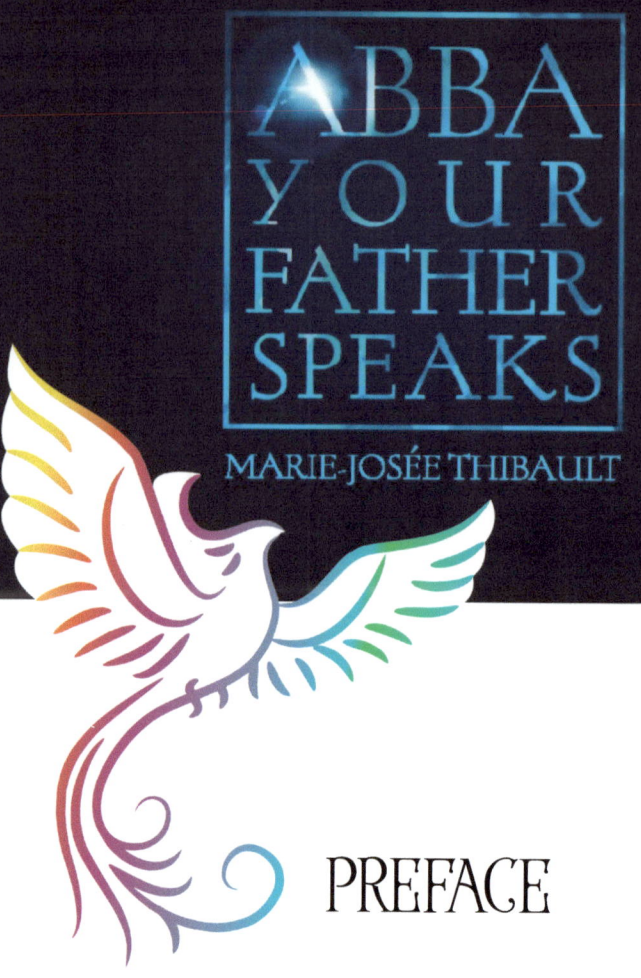

PREFACE

I wrote this wonderful and miraculous book because I was ordered to do so directly by God, the Father Almighty. My mission on Earth, which was revealed to me by the Father, Himself, is clear: I am the essence of Saint Paul. I will serve the Lord every day of my life and spread the teachings I receive from Heaven. Jesus, I trust in you. In Christ, we are One. In the blue mantle of our Blessed Divine Mother, our Virgin Mary, I dwell and pray. All honor and glory to God, forever and ever! Amen. Alleluia!

This book was written solely by Abba Father, Himself, word for word. I took these Divine Words in dictation in a sacred, reverential manner. Woe unto me if the Father's Golden Word is tarnished in the least. Abba Father deeply desires a unique, one-on-one, and awe-inspiring relationship with every creature of His creation.

He loves you so much, each one of you. Love Him back. Only in Heaven will you understand the infinite gift hidden in these words, full of His Graces. Sacred Heart of Jesus, have mercy on us. In the immaculate Heart of my Sweet Divine Mother, my Virgin Mary, I dwell and pray. Glory to God in the highest, and on Earth, peace to men of goodwill. Amen. Alleluia!

Marie-Josée Thibault

FREE DOWNLOAD

Get your free copy of :
"Dear Humanity: Book 1"
when you sign up to the
author's VIP mailing list!
Get started here:

www.abbamyfatheriloveyou.com

I AM

1 My children of the earth, listen to Me well. The end times are drawing near. ²My Judgment, that is to say, the Judgment of God, the Father Almighty, will befall the earth very shortly. ³I have sent many messengers throughout history in order to show you the way toward Me. ⁴My Son, Christ Jesus, My Meek Lamb of Redemption, has been, is, and always will be My messenger of the Most High. ⁵The Most Blessed and Most Sweet Virgin Mary, physical Mother of My Son during His journey on earth, is also a messenger-servant, whose

Powers are extraordinarily more important than you can imagine. ⁶The Saints in Paradise, who are speaking to you through this collection, are also My beloved messengers. ⁷My Voice—the Voice of the Eternal and Almighty Father, the Voice of your Creator, the Voice of the Creator of all things visible and invisible on earth, the Supreme Governor of all the souls inhabiting the earth—My Voice thus is communicated to you through Marie-Josée T., My daughter chosen to be a vessel of My Grace, and this since the Creation of the world. ⁸For Marie-Josée is the essence of Saint Paul, the Logos of the conversion to Christ Jesus. ⁹Christ Jesus of Nazareth, My Redeemer Lamb, is the One and Only Way bringing you back to Me. ¹⁰I bring everything back to Me; everything, absolutely everything that I created, will return to Me. ¹¹I am the Eternal and Almighty Father, and I love you. ¹²My dear children, I am speaking to you today because this is pleasant to Me. ¹³I am God, the Father Almighty, Creator of all things visible and invisible, and nothing can be taken away from Me; nothing can be given to Me; nothing can alter the Love That I Am; nothing can change He Who Is. ¹⁴I am God, and I rule over all the souls inhabiting the earth, as well as those inhabiting the rest of the universe. ¹⁵Nothing escapes Me;

nothing unfolds outside of Me; nothing can exist unless My Will so desires. ¹⁶For I am God, the Creator of the world, and everything belongs to Me. ¹⁷I am the Father of the Son; I am the Father of all souls, and I act as a Father must act (according to your human understanding of that term). ¹⁸It is important, dear soul, that I clarify here the reason for My conversation with you. Dear little soul who will live shortly the horrors of the end times, I lean toward you in order to prepare you to meet Me personally. ¹⁹For shortly, very shortly, My Judgment on earth will befall. I love you.

Pray

YOU

2 My dear children, listen to Me well. I am your Father in Heaven, God, the Father Almighty. ²The life you are living on earth is infinitely brief, the duration of lightning, truly. ³This life animating you is the result of My Divine and Merciful Will, not the result of favorable chemical reactions. ⁴The Fire of Life animating you derives from the Divine Fire of the Central Sun, which is the Cradle of Creation. I will later explain the nature of the Central Sun. ⁵For today, dear child whom I love, be assured of My Love and of My Mercy on your soul, which belongs to Me exclusively. ⁶For all life on earth unfolds according to My Divine Will, which is at once Infinite Justice and Infinite Mercy, and My Reign over Creation will never end since I have decided so. I love you. ⁷My beloved children on earth, listen to Me well. The life I gave you, though brief, is of paramount importance to Me. ⁸I want to see all the souls I have created return peacefully into My Arms. ⁹However, evil has infiltrated the earth, and many of My children have abandoned the peaceful road bringing them back to Me and have chosen instead the dangerous road leading to Satan. ¹⁰Such error! Such offense made against My Heart of Father! Such sin that must be paid in the future! ¹¹For every offense committed against Me, your Father, your God, your Creator, represents a firm debt that must be paid sooner or later. ¹²I will explain later, dear hearts, how to pay your debts toward Me. ¹³For you all have debts toward Me—oh yes! ¹⁴Today, My little soul that I created with My own Hands, I want you to say to Me the Lord's Prayer as often as possible, in a way never done before. ¹⁵Know that this prayer is pleasing to Me at the highest point. ¹⁶Know that

I conceived this prayer Myself, and after having transmitted it to My Son, I charged Him to offer it to humanity for its global redemption. [17]Know that I hear all the Lord's Prayers—the same way that I hear all your thoughts and words, even the most intimate and the most villainous ones, each one of you inhabiting the earth, regardless of your belief in Me. [18]For you all live in Me, and I carry you all within Myself. [19]Pray, My children, pray often today to Me, your Father, your God, your Creator, and say the Lord's Prayer with love, conviction, and sincerity. [20]And this will be pleasing to Me. I love you.

PRAY

3 My children, My dear children whom I love, pray to Me; pray day and night; pray with tears and fervor; pray and implore me again. ²For yes, My beloved children, I hear all your prayers, little ones and great ones, those made in the silence of your hearts, those sung at the time of liturgical gathering in Church, and those made in the intimacy of your daily activities. ³I order you to pray to Me more often, dear hearts, for this command is written in the Gospels, and the praying heart draws near to Me considerably, and this is pleasing to Me. ⁴Pray about everything at all times, regarding your personal comfort, as well as the major problems of humanity and all creatures of the earth. ⁵Pray for health at all levels of your body, as well as for those whom you carry in your heart. ⁶Pray for all those whom you meet and who are seeking Me (more or less consciously). ⁷Pray and thank Me for everything that you are, for everything that you have, for everything that humanity uses to operate because in fact, it is My Grace that wills it, and everything existing on earth is loaned to you, not given. ⁸Pray harder; pray more deeply; pray more frequently; pray more sincerely. ⁹Pray regarding everything happening in your life and for humanity. ¹⁰Pray for the dead (I will explain this in more detail later). ¹¹Pray and speak to Me constantly, for this is pleasing to Me — and pleasing Me should be the primary goal of your life. I love you. ¹²My dear children, do not delay your approach toward Me. ¹³I say unto you, I say unto you verily, the end times are drawing near, very very much so. ¹⁴He Who has the Power over your life and especially over your soul, your Father, your God, your Creator, is speaking to you today, for it is pleasing to Me to give you Mercy. ¹⁵You are reading these Words, for My beloved

and chosen child, Marie-Josée T., hears My Voice by the grace of clairaudience that I gave her, according to My Divine Will that is now encompassing you. [16]Be in a state of deep gratitude toward Me for My Blessing upon your soul today. [17]Be in a state of constant prayer as My Apostle of Redemption, Saint Paul, taught you. [18]Be in a state of universal charity toward all the souls around you—humans, animals, and plants. [19]For what you do unto each of My creatures of My Creation, you do unto Me, Who am Love itself. [20]Any act that is opposed to an act of charity is a direct offense against Me, and this offense accumulates and generates a debt toward Me. [21]I will teach you, dear heart, what represents your debt toward Me. [22]For now, My child, come into My Arms full of Love for you; come into My Benevolent Arms of Father, and say to Me the most beautiful Lord's Prayer of your life:

[23]Our Father, Who Art in Heaven,

Hallowed be Thy Name.

Thy Kingdom come.

Thy Will be done

on earth as it is in Heaven.

Give us this day our daily bread.

Forgive us our trespasses,

as we forgive those who trespass against us,

and lead us not into temptation,

but deliver us from evil.

Amen.

I love you.

CHRIST JESUS OF NAZARETH

4 My children, My dearest children of the earth, listen to Me well. Today, more than ever, more than any other time in your life so far, I desire to hold your soul in My Hands. ²By this, I mean that I want to see a concrete outpouring of your soul toward Me according to your own individual and personal will. ³I want to hear the most beautiful prayers of your life addressed to Me directly. ⁴I want to see your spiritual disposition open for Me like never before. ⁵I want to feel your heart spring up toward Me and beat for no one else but Me, your Creator and your God. ⁶I want to hear your sighs and your intimate pleas for My Divine Mercy, for My Divine Mercy is everything you need in your earthly life in order to present yourself to Me pure and white as snow at the time of passage that is death. ⁷Life on earth is infected by evil; I am the Only One Who can deliver you from evil. ⁸That is why I sent you My Beloved Son, My Redeemer Lamb, My Way toward Me, your Unique Salvation, Christ Jesus of Nazareth. ⁹Listen to Him, for He speaks to you in your heart, far more often than you might imagine, and His Words are written in the Golden Book that is the Truth, the True Knowledge of Me, He Who Is, your Creator and your God. I love you.

MY DIVINE WILL

5 My children, My dearest beloved children, listen to Me well. Life on earth, dear hearts, lasts only the time of lightning. ²Immediately at the birth of a human being on earth, according to My Precise and Immutable Divine Will, promptly the process of future and inevitable death is engaged, and this, again and always according to My Precise and Immutable Divine Will. ³My Divine Will, dear children, rules your life, regardless of your belief in Me or in what you call the religious domain. ⁴For I am God the Father

Almighty, your Creator and your God, and all things visible and invisible belong to Me since I have created everything, in the same manner that I am creating this moment between you and Me, dear little soul in My Hands, at this moment when I am speaking to you. [5]I have created everything, and I will continue to create everything, from moment to moment and for Eternity. [6]And I command life or death to all the souls that I created in the physical and tridimensional plane that you know, according to My Personal and Divine Will. [7]Nothing escapes Me, as you know, since My entire Creation lives in Me, and nothing unfolds herein unless My Divine and Absolute Will so desires. [8]Time elapses quickly on earth; I repeat it; look back and consider the length of your life so far. [9]By this, dear child, I want to inspire you to accelerate your approach toward Me and to transform your human steps into giant steps, in such a manner that I see and feel leaps and bounds toward Me from you, cosmic and gigantic leaps and bounds, like you have never done before. [10]For the end times are near, dear souls, and you are left with very very little time to reach Me in My Heart of Father. I love you. [11]My children, My dearest beloved

Marie-Josée Thibault

children, listen to Me well. Life on earth is much easier, more comfortable, and happier when you have deep faith in Me. ¹²I am He Who decides and sanctions the trials experienced by each one of you during your life. ¹³I am also He Who is responsible for removing these trials, if it is pleasing to Me, according to My Divine and Absolute Will. ¹⁴The trials that I am sending you, My dear hearts, are intended to edify your souls, strengthen your faith, and force you to pray — the golden way toward Me. ¹⁵Yes, My children, you are obligated to pray to Me because it is taught in the Gospels and because it will allow you to draw considerably closer to Me. ¹⁶Prayer keeps away evil; prayer helps you pay your debts toward Me; prayer puts you in constant contact with Me, your Creator, your Father, and your God. ¹⁷Most of all, prayer helps strengthen your faith in Me and ultimately make your life on earth more comfortable. ¹⁸Is it not more comfortable to be healthy than to be sick? ¹⁹To have a full stomach than an empty stomach? ²⁰To function in society rather than being rejected by society? ²¹I desire to see your soul grand and beautiful among the other souls who walk the earth, putting into practice the gifts and talents that I have personally assigned to you and helping spread the Good News of the Kingdom of Heaven on earth. ²²For this is your only social goal: to spread My Divine Word. I love you.

HEAVEN

6 My children, My dearest children of the earth, listen to Me well. Life on earth is short; I have already said so, but Life in the Kingdom of Heaven, the Paradise awaiting you at the end of your life, is Eternal. ²You cannot imagine, dear children, dear hearts, the beauty, the greatness, and the magnificence of the Paradise I created, and this at the time of Genesis, the Cradle of the universe. ³The Saints in Paradise have mentioned it in the other books transcribed by Marie-Josée. ⁴Suffice for Me to tell you, dear little soul in My Hands, the Hands of your Father, your God, your Creator, that I personally invite you to join Me here in My House, which is your House, after the passage that is death. ⁵Your soul will be white as snow and you will merit Heaven if you put into practice the teachings given by My Son, Christ Jesus of Nazareth, and the other messengers I have sent you throughout the history of humanity. ⁶For your soul must be purified before being admitted to Paradise. ⁷I will draw closer to your little soul wandering on earth, dear child, and I will make it beautiful and grand in My own Way, like a father acts toward his beloved child. ⁸Be prepared, vigilant, and in constant prayer, for your life will shortly take a new course since I made it My Decision. ⁹I bless you, and I love you.

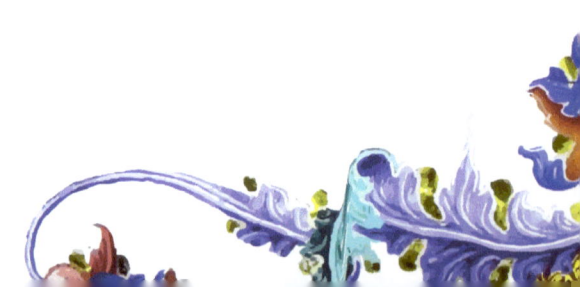

LOVE

7 My children, My dearest children, listen to Me well. Today, more than any other day of your life so far, I desire to see your soul in a state of incomparable purity. ²Know that today, at the very moment you are reading these lines—the moment that I have chosen Myself since I bring everything back to Me in My own Way—My Divine Mercy is spreading within your soul. ³I desire to see your soul in a state of boundless receptivity to My Spirit. ⁴I desire to see your heart wide open so that I can pour forth My Graces within it. ⁵I desire to see your oneself

rendered very little, very humble, and very simple so as not to offer Me any resistance of any kind – do not block Me! ⁶I have strewn your life with many trials in order to bring you to this point, at this moment when I am speaking to you, and nothing unfolding in your life has taken place outside My Precise and Supreme Will. ⁷Know that I carry you in My Heart of Father and that this same Heart of Father will never cease to love you, to forgive you, to be patient and flexible with you, to be moved by your prayers and your tears, and especially to be strict when you wander into evil. ⁸For I bring you back to Me in My own Way, I repeat it unto you, and your soul must be purified of all sins and mistakes you have committed against Me and men during your life. ⁹I know them all—the most minute ones, as well as the most perverse ones—and only I can give you the forgiveness of all sins and the resulting purification. ¹⁰Today, dear little soul, show Me your soul pious, virtuous, repentant, and above all, white as snow, for My Divine Mercy is spreading within your soul to the same extent that the state of purity is found therein. ¹¹I will help you. I bless you, and I love you. ¹²My children, My dearest children,

listen to Me well. Today, more than any other moment in your life, I desire to see your heart ascend to Heaven in order to join the Holy Spirit Who will descend unto you. [13]The Holy Spirit, My dear child, is the Spirit of God, the Spirit of the Holy Trinity Who is the One and Only God, My Spirit. [14]Verily, verily I say unto you, My Spirit will descend unto you, in the exact measure that your heart will ascend toward Him, according to the interior and spiritual movements of your soul seeking Me. [15]Be in a state of deep inner recollection; be in a state of purity of the Spirit. [16]Feel light as a feather, without the past, without sin, without worries, and let your consciousness float gently over your body and well beyond this vile earth. [17]I will respond immediately and personally to the motion of your soul by making My Consoling Spirit descend unto it. [18]Then, you will understand why it is said that the Holy Spirit, the Spirit of God, is Love. I love you.

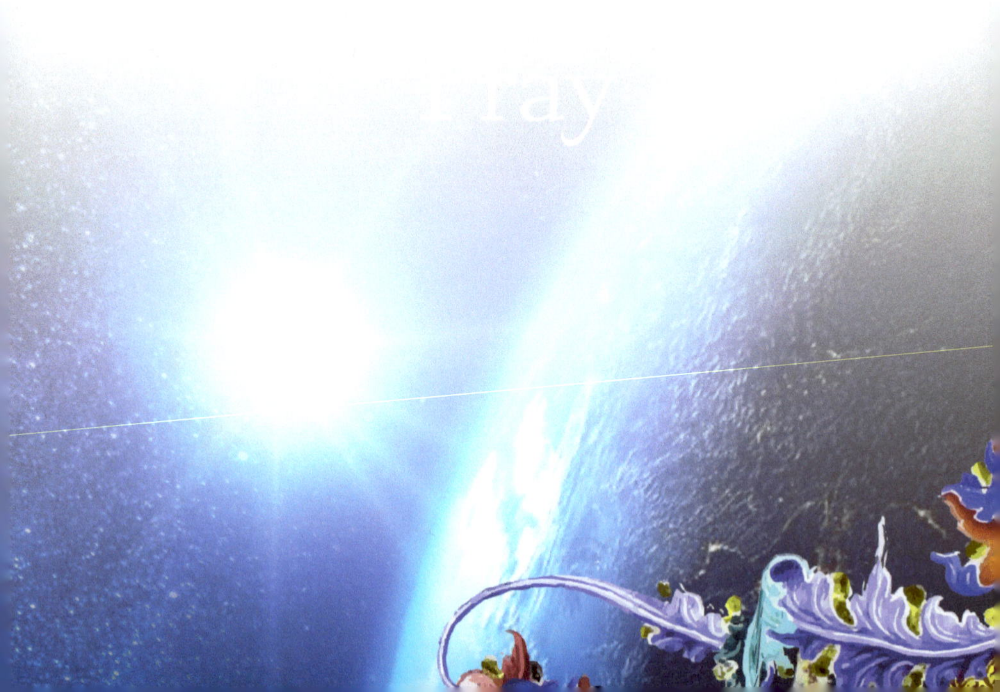

Pray

MY OWN WAY

8 My children, My dearest children, today do not be under the influence of the devil. ²The devil, My beloved ones, truly exists, and its harmful and evil effects are felt on the entire earth. ³Unfortunately, as you can see for yourself, evil on earth has spread at an alarming and shocking rate. ⁴The behavior of a very large number of My children offends Me immeasurably. ⁵I will speak later of My Great Plan of Purification of the earth. ⁶For today, dear heart, say no to anything that is not of Christ as you know Him. ⁷For Christ Jesus of Nazareth, My Beloved Son, is the Way, the Truth, and the Life, and no one else but Him can lead you to Me. I love you. ⁸My dear children, My dearest beloved children, listen to Me well. Today I am announcing with great sorrow the difficult times that are at your door. ⁹I say unto you, I say unto you verily, the end times are near, for reasons that I will explain today. ¹⁰My children, evil has infested the earth. ¹¹You know it; you see it, but My observation of the abyss of evil that has become the earth is more complete and more detailed than you can imagine. ¹²Satan, My foe, has wreaked havoc in your hearts and bodies; consequently, your souls have become hideously sullen. ¹³No impure soul can enter Paradise, for only purity and My Grace live herein. ¹⁴Thus, dear soul in distress, you cannot return to My House before My purification process takes place within your soul and by extension, in all the souls who live on planet Earth. ¹⁵I know perfectly well the current state of your soul and what is beneficial to make it white as snow. ¹⁶I also know perfectly well the current state of all collective souls on earth. ¹⁷Thus, the events that are fast approaching will be processes of embellishment and purifica-

Marie-Josée Thibault

tion of your soul—and of all the souls on earth—for no other remedy against evil that has infiltrated therein will be able to destroy the enemy. [18]I desire to see your soul as white as snow; I have already said so, and I repeat it. [19]I will proceed with the purification of your soul in My own Way and at the time of My choice. [20]For My Divine Will is Supreme, and I decide everything regarding all the souls inhabiting the earth, and this at all times. I love you.

JOHN THE BAPTIST

9 My children, My dearest children, listen to Me well. The horrors to come have nothing to do with the Mayan prophecies or with some other calculations originating from ancient civilizations. Of course not! ²The end times that are fast approaching are the result of My Divine Will, Supreme and Immutable. ³I alone decide on the magnitude, the nature, and the timing of the events to come. ⁴For the end times are written in My Great Plan of Purification of humanity. ⁵And to that end, My role as Father forces Me to carry out the purification and edification of the souls of all My children. ⁶I am sorrowful and often shocked and offended by the barbarisms, the cruelties, and the infamies of far too many of My children. ⁷Materialism, which hardens and becomes more perverted day by day, has spread all over the earth, even where I was hoping to see endure a beautiful and mystical tradition sheltered away from the vain and futile temptations of the world. ⁸My disappointment becomes heavier every day to the same degree as your debts toward Me become heavier, and at the sight of such evil widespread on earth, I have no choice but to proceed with very large and very deep cleaning of all the souls inhabiting the earth. I love you. ⁹My children, My dearest children, listen to Me well. Clearly, your souls must be cleansed of all impurities. ¹⁰It is also clear that the time has come for thorough cleaning of all the souls inhabiting the earth. ¹¹Are you asking Me, "Why now?" ¹²This question cannot be answered without spiritual maturity of the soul, bringing about intelligence and fortitude when the Truth is spoken. ¹³At this point in your life, I cannot answer it. ¹⁴However, I assure you that shortly, very shortly, your soul will be awakened enough to hear and understand the Truth. [15]Meanwhile, dear hearts, be in a state of vigilance and preparedness at all levels. [16]Signs at the social level will be given: hatred will be of unparalleled cruelty; people will kill one another for a coin; and the birds will fall from the sky, struck by death. [17]Know, My beloved children, that the creatures of the sky are My favorite creatures in the animal Kingdom and that they all wake up in Heaven with Me after the passage that is death. [18]It is the same with all the creatures of all My Kingdoms — except the human race. [19]For any debt against Me has to be paid in full before a soul is declared pure in My Eyes. [20]Go today, My children, in the spiritual disposition of the greatest Saint, John the Baptist, and prepare the way for the Lord Redeemer, My Beloved Son, Jesus Christ of Nazareth. I love you.

Pray

ON EARTH

10 My children, My dearest children of the earth, listen to Me well. This message on My behalf was brief. ²However, be assured of My periodic messages through Marie-Josée T., the essence of Saint Paul on earth, whom I have chosen as a vessel of My grace. ³Woe to them who touch her, woe to them who blaspheme her, woe to them who do not believe these Words that My Mercy grants you. ⁴For I am God the Father Almighty, your Creator and your God, and I have Supreme Sovereignty over all the souls on earth, believers and unbelievers, and I will be without Mercy for those who attack My messenger on earth. ⁵I will speak again to you very soon. ⁶Be in constant prayer. ⁷I bless you, and I love you.

Abba, your Father

AFTERWORD

Abba, your Father, Speaks? You mean, Our Father can speak? Yes, Marie-Josée is clairvoyant and clairaudient and has been chosen by Our Father Himself to be a vessel of His Grace. Let God the Father Almighty take hold of your soul in His Heart, and you shall reach the last page, mysteriously transformed. This short book is nothing less than an epiphany.

Abba Father loves you, for He says so, and He does so—mightily. Draw closer to Him by reading Book I, the first installment of the Abba Books series.

Praised be Jesus Christ, our Savior, and our God. Amen. Alleluia!

ABOUT THE AUTHOR

Marie-Josée Thibault's life is in no way similar to yours. When she wakes, the saints of Heaven visit her, talk to her, teach her, and pray intensely with her. When such mystical sessions draw to a close, she greets with great respect and deep reverence the Masters of the Heavenly Court. This servant of the Lord spends the rest of the day in the company of her guardian angel, who continues her spiritual education and ceaselessly protects her from the perils of this fallen world. Bestowed by the Heavenly Father, her gifts of clairvoyance and clairaudience allow her to remain in continuous contact with the supernatural dimension juxtaposed with ours, where the soul is born of the Spirit through Jesus and Mary. She prays that, one day soon, the entire human race will give glory to the Father, the Son, and the Holy Spirit.

Also by Marie-Josée Thibault

Abba, your Father, Speaks: Book II

Saint Padre Pio Speaks: Tome I

Dear Humanity: Book I & II

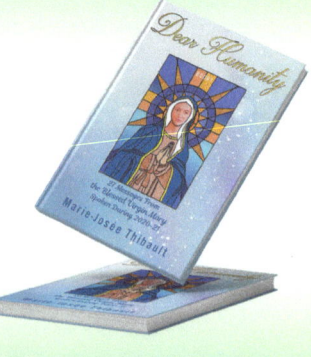

FREE DOWNLOAD

Get your free copy of : "Dear Humanity: Book 1" when you sign up to the author's VIP mailing list! Get started here:

www.abbamyfatheriloveyou.com

www.ingramcontent.com/pod-product-compliance
Lightning Source LLC
Chambersburg PA
CBHW041623220426
43662CB00001B/32